PIANO • VOCAL • GUITAR

the best of The Beatles
25 greatest hits

CONTENTS

2	All You Need Is Love
10	Can't Buy Me Love
7	Come Together
14	Day Tripper
18	Eight Days A Week
24	Eleanor Rigby
22	Get Back
27	Hard Day's Night, A
32	Hello, Goodbye
36	Help!
40	Hey Jude
52	I Feel Fine
44	I Want To Hold Your Hand
48	Lady Madonna
55	Let It Be
60	Long And Winding Road, The
64	Love Me Do
72	Paperback Writer
67	Penny Lane
76	Please Please Me
79	She Loves You
88	Something
84	Ticket To Ride
91	We Can Work It Out
94	Yesterday

This publication is not for sale in
the E.C. and/or Australia
or New Zealand.

7777 W. BLUEMOUND RD. P.O. BOX 10019 MILWAUKEE, WI 53213

For all works contained herein:
Unauthorized copying, arranging, adapting, recording or public performance is an infringement of copyright.
Infringers are liable under the law.

COME TOGETHER

Moderately slow, with a double-time feeling

Words and Music by
JOHN LENNON and PAUL McCARTNEY

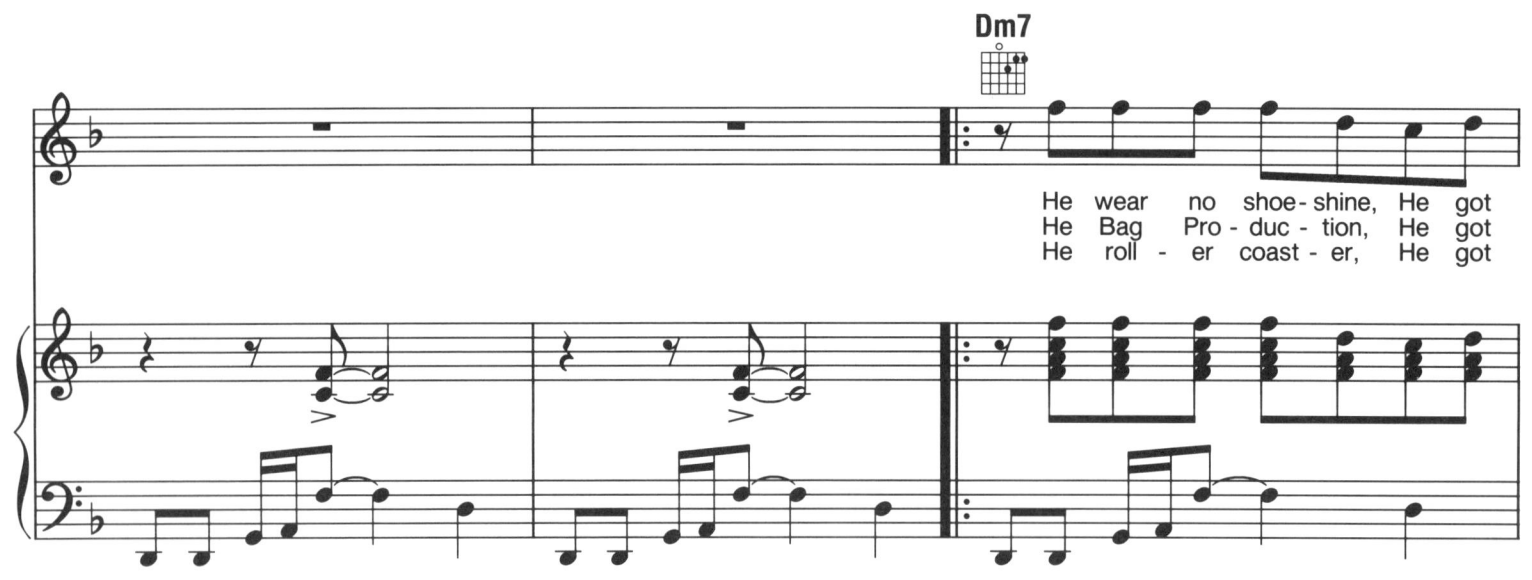
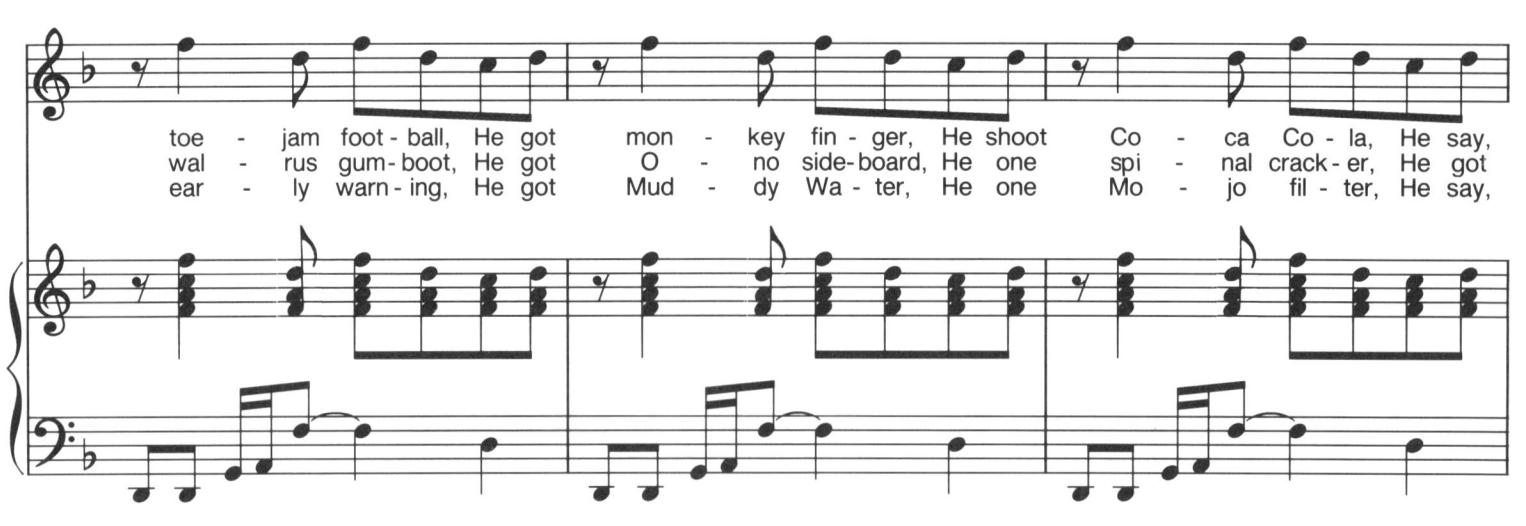

DAY TRIPPER

Words and Music by
JOHN LENNON and PAUL McCARTNEY

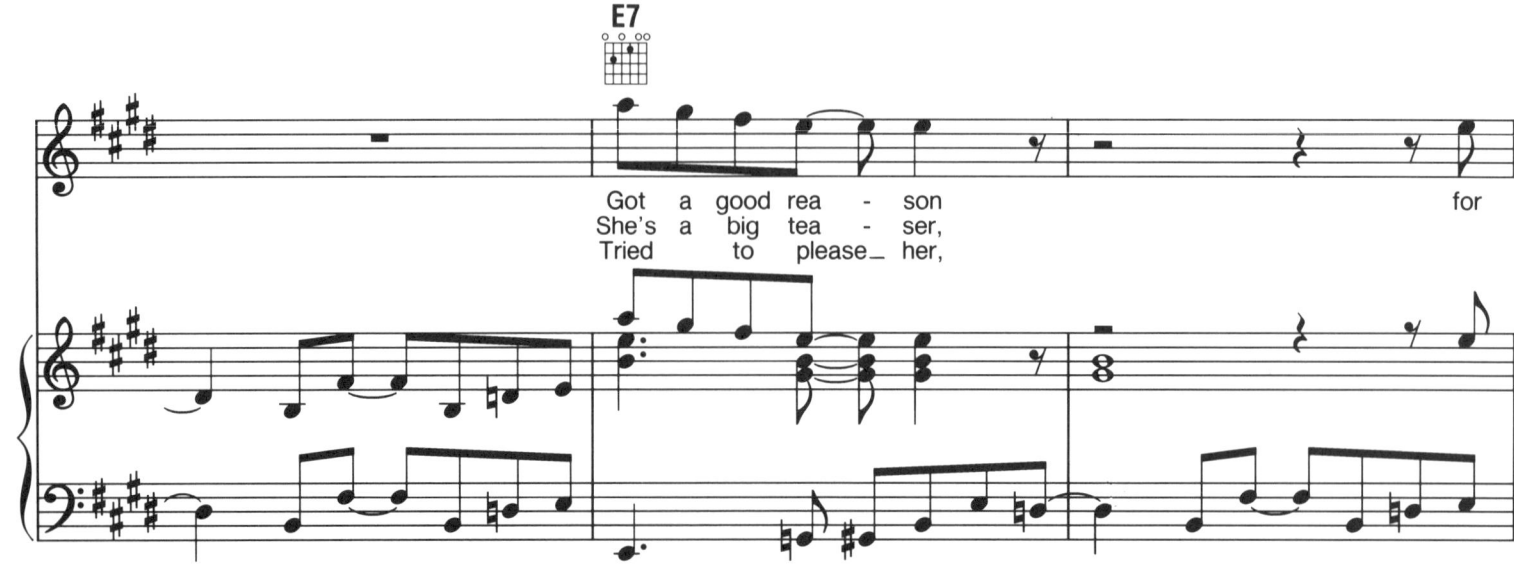

Got a good rea-son   for
She's a big tea-ser,
Tried to please_ her,

Copyright © 1965 NORTHERN SONGS LIMITED
All Rights Administered by BLACKWOOD MUSIC INC. under license from ATV MUSIC (MACLEN)
All Rights Reserved   International Copyright Secured

EIGHT DAYS A WEEK

Words and Music by
JOHN LENNON and PAUL McCARTNEY

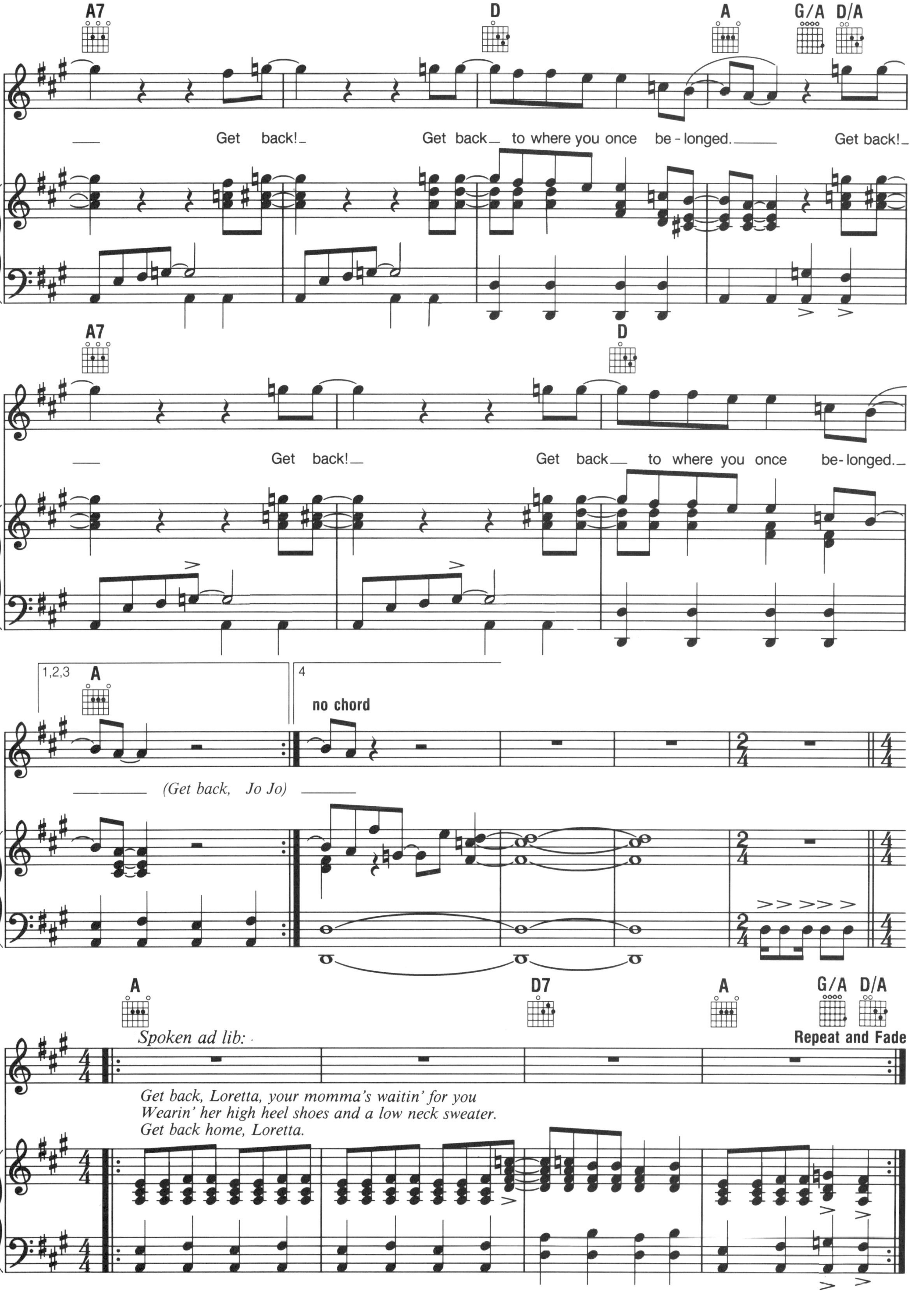
A7
D
A
G/A
D/A
Get back!
Get back to where you once be-longed.
Get back!
A7
D
Get back!
Get back to where you once be-longed.
1,2,3
A
4
no chord
(Get back, Jo Jo)
A
D7
A
G/A
D/A
Spoken ad lib:
Repeat and Fade
Get back, Loretta, your momma's waitin' for you
Wearin' her high heel shoes and a low neck sweater.
Get back home, Loretta.

ELEANOR RIGBY

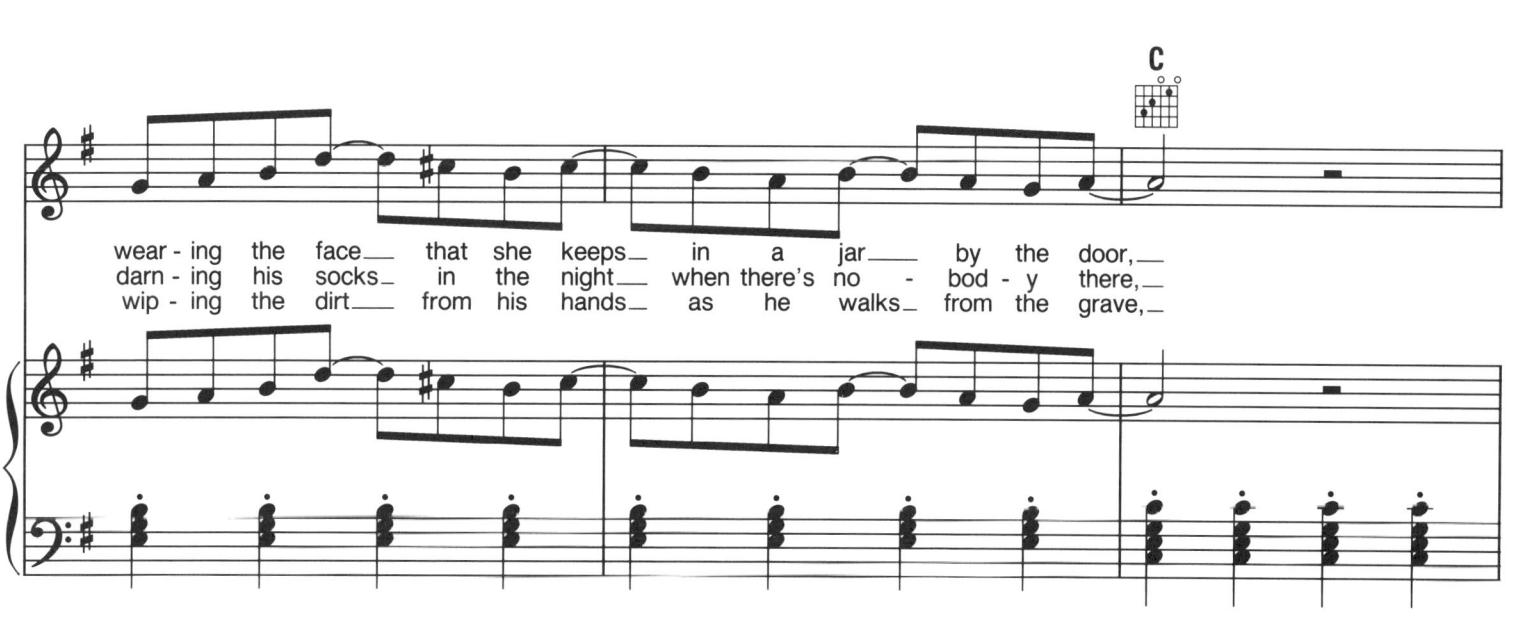

A HARD DAY'S NIGHT

Words and Music by
JOHN LENNON and PAUL McCARTNEY

HELLO, GOODBYE

Words and Music by
JOHN LENNON and PAUL McCARTNEY

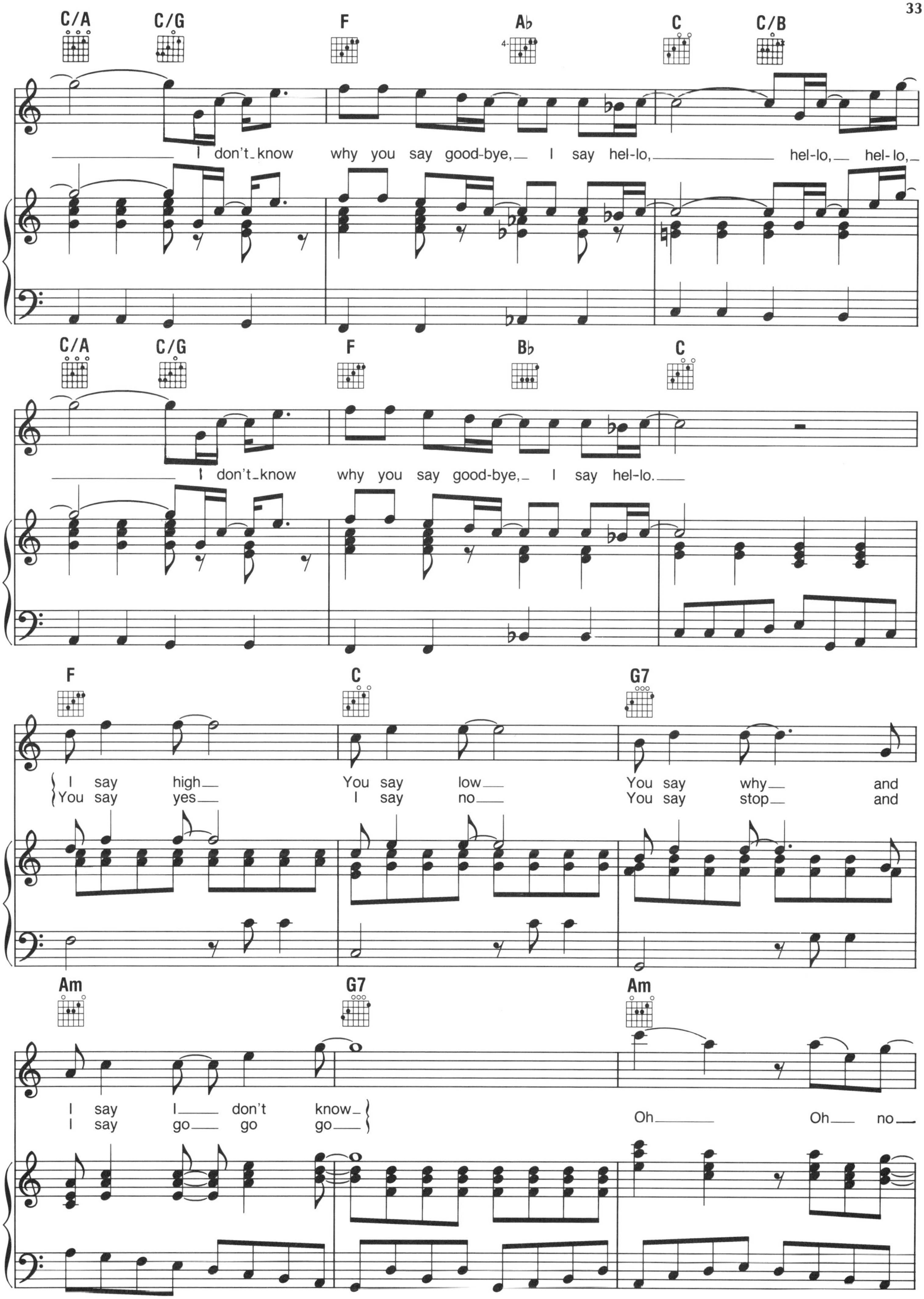
C/A C/G F A♭ C C/B
I don't know why you say good-bye, I say hel-lo, hel-lo, hel-lo,
C/A C/G F B♭ C
I don't know why you say good-bye, I say hel-lo.
F C G7
I say high You say low You say why and
You say yes I say no You say stop and
Am G7 Am
I say I don't know
I say go go go
Oh Oh no

HELP!

HEY JUDE

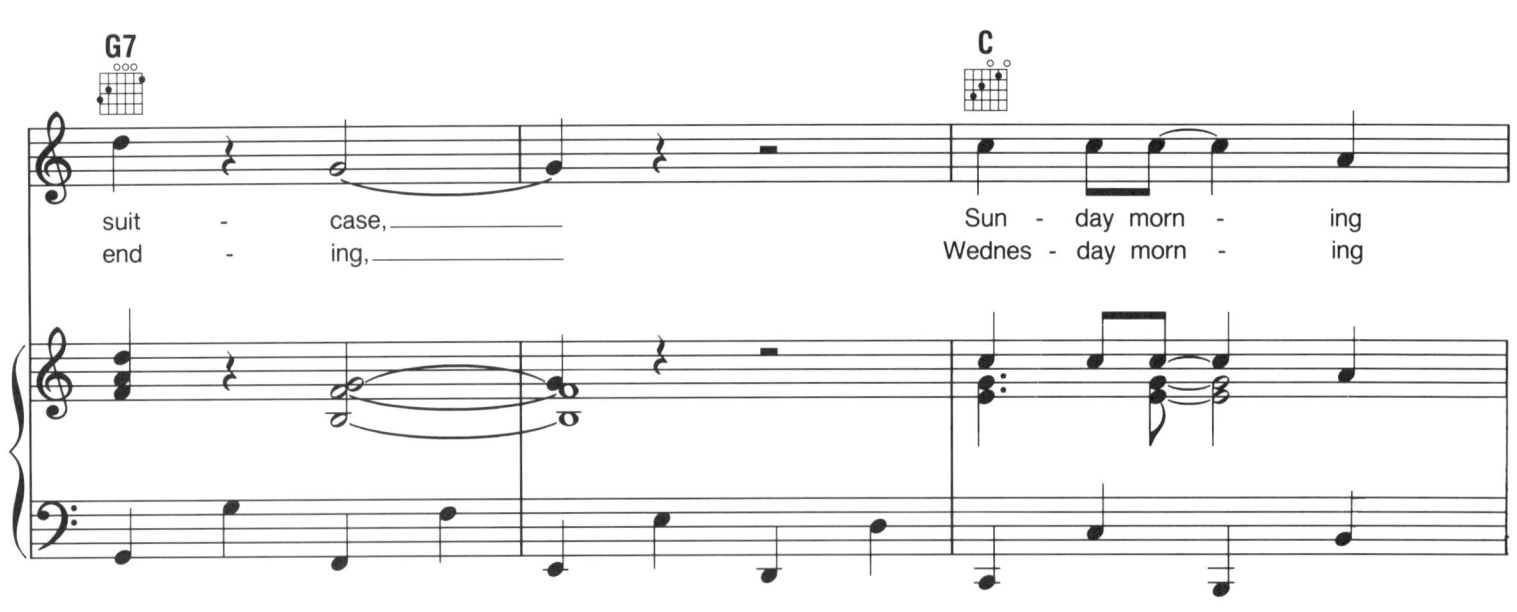

I FEEL FINE

Words and Music by
JOHN LENNON and PAUL McCARTNEY

THE LONG AND WINDING ROAD

Words and Music by JOHN LENNON and PAUL McCARTNEY

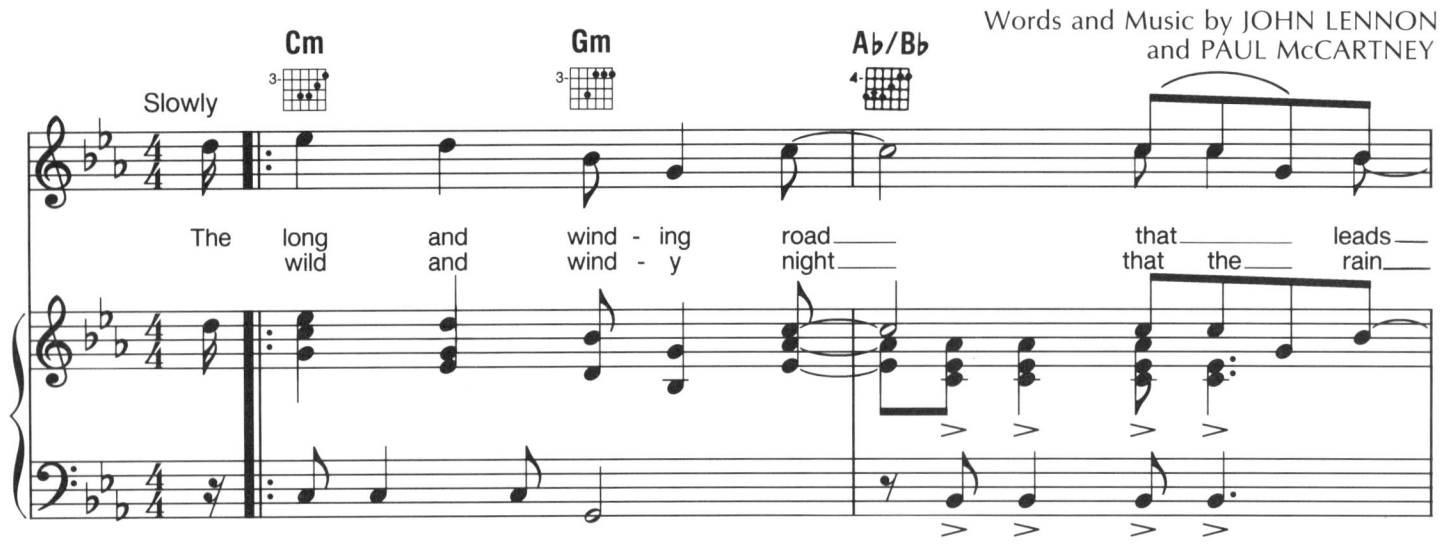
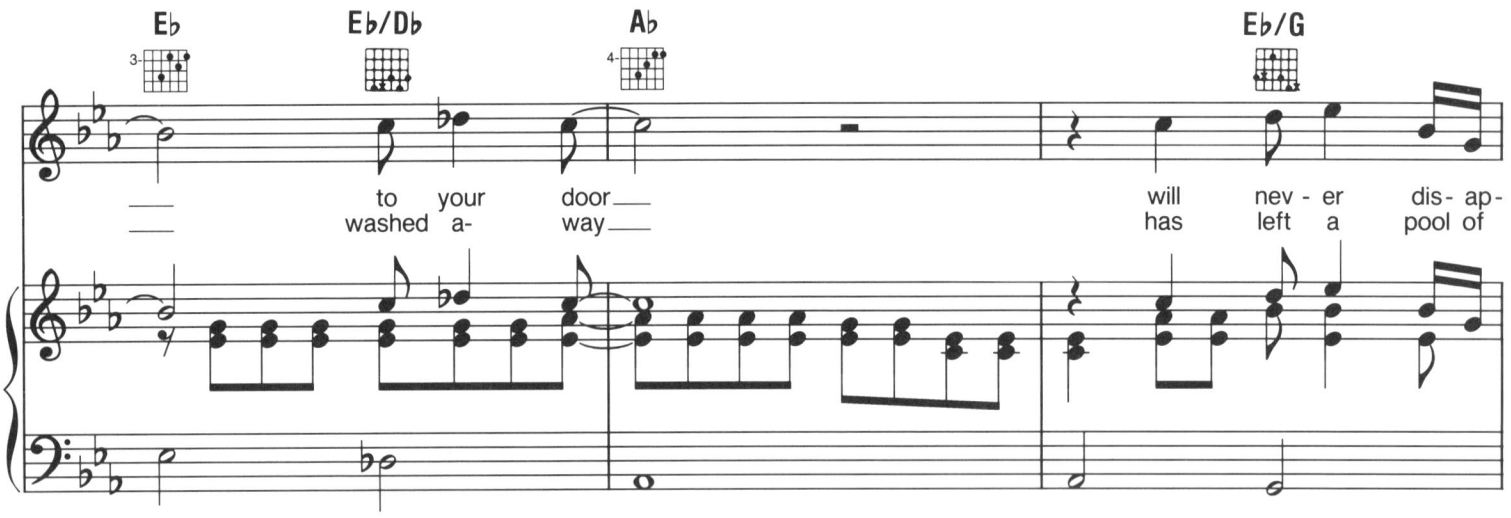

Copyright © 1970 NORTHERN SONGS LIMITED
All Rights Administered by BLACKWOOD MUSIC INC. under license from ATV MUSIC (MACLEN)
All Rights Reserved   International Copyright Secured

man-y ways I've tried. And still they lead me back to the long winding road.

You left me standing here a long, long time a-go.

LOVE ME DO

~~65~~

PENNY LANE

58 tempo 109
Function - Transpose -3

Words and Music by JOHN LENNON
and PAUL McCARTNEY

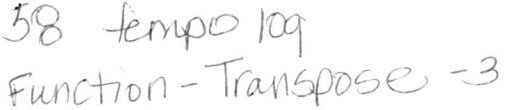

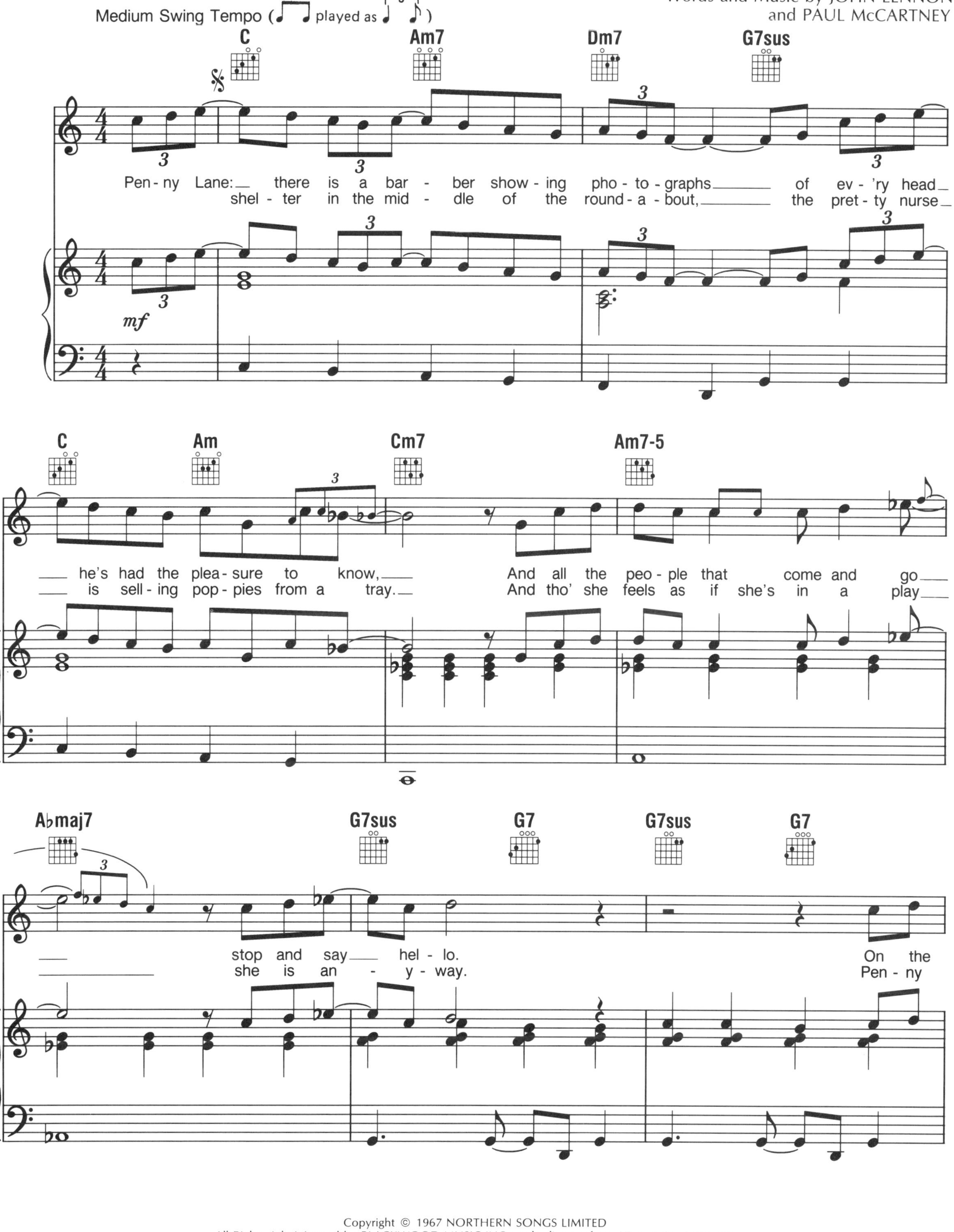

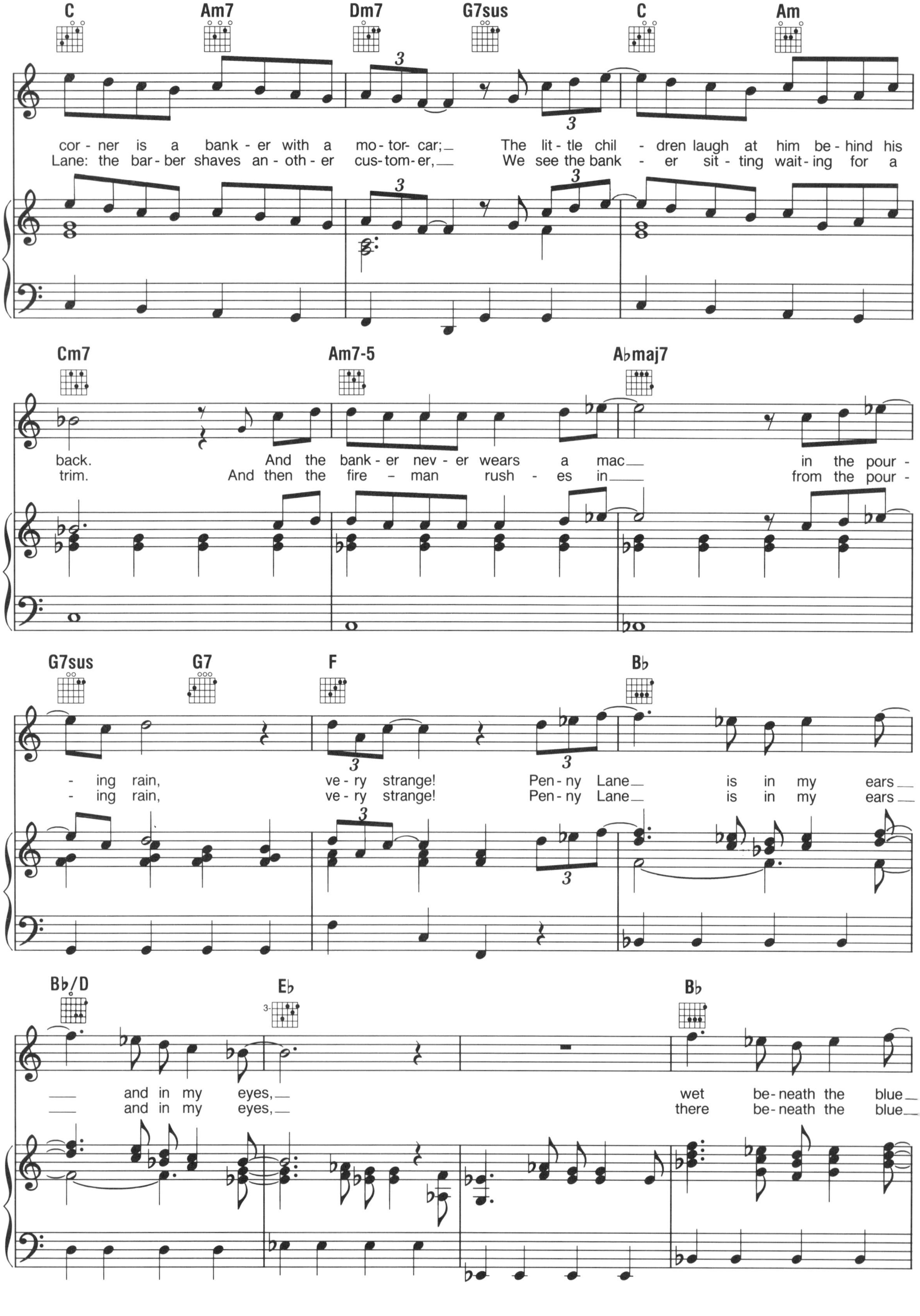
C Am7 Dm7 G7sus C Am
cor - ner is a bank - er with a mo - tor - car; The lit - tle chil - dren laugh at him be - hind his
Lane: the bar - ber shaves an - oth - er cus - tom - er, We see the bank - er sit - ting wait - ing for a
3
Cm7 Am7-5 A♭maj7
back. And the bank - er nev - er wears a mac in the pour -
trim. And then the fire - man rush - es in from the pour -
G7sus G7 F B♭
- ing rain, ve - ry strange! Pen - ny Lane is in my ears
- ing rain, ve - ry strange! Pen - ny Lane is in my ears
B♭/D E♭ B♭
and in my eyes, wet be - neath the blue
and in my eyes, there be - neath the blue

PAPERBACK WRITER

Words and Music by
JOHN LENNON and PAUL McCARTNEY

SHE LOVES YOU

82

TICKET TO RIDE

SOMETHING

Words and Music by
GEORGE HARRISON

WE CAN WORK IT OUT

YESTERDAY

Words and Music by JOHN LENNON
and PAUL McCARTNEY

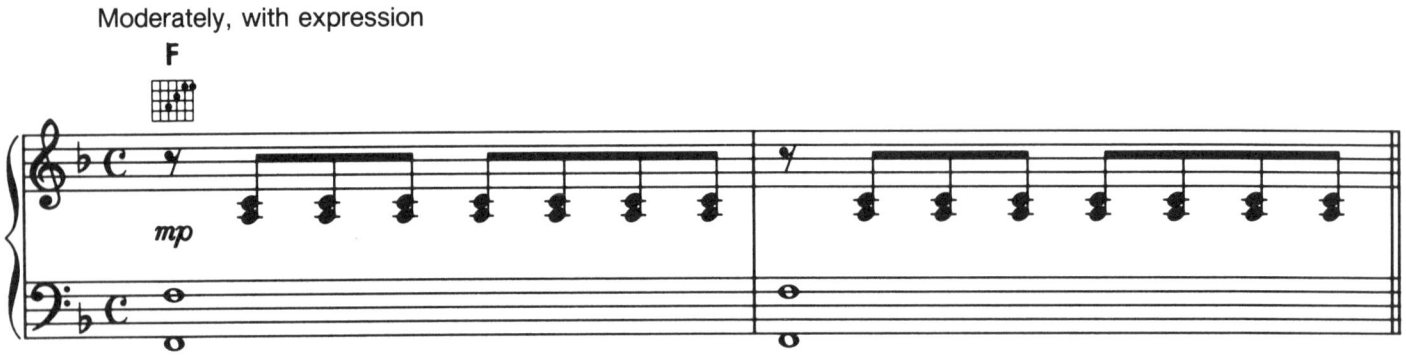
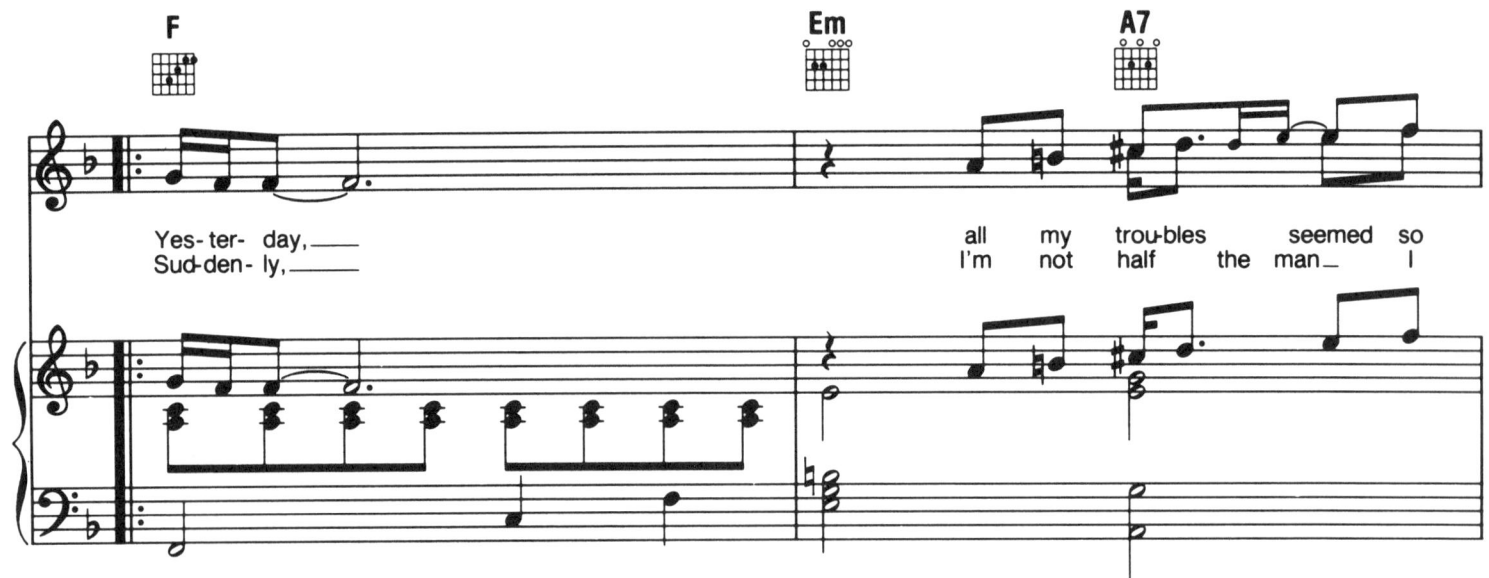

Yes-ter-day,___ all my trou-bles seemed so far a-way,___ Now it looks as though___ they're
Sud-den-ly,___ I'm not half the man___ I used to be, There's a sha-dow hang-ing

Copyright © 1965 NORTHERN SONGS LIMITED
All Rights Administered by BLACKWOOD MUSIC INC. under license from ATV MUSIC (MACLEN)
All Rights Reserved   International Copyright Secured